Learn To Drive Complete Version

A Complete & Comprehensive Guide For Learning to Drive.

Joseph Collins. ADI.

Second Edition

Cover Design & Illustrations by Jane Maguire

Introduction

This book includes both my other books; **'Learn to Drive (General Driving)'** & **'Learn To Drive (All the Manoeuvres)'** and has an extra seven exercises that will complete your driving knowledge in full depth, after all you have to be able to deal with every aspects of driving eventually. They are:

Pedestrian Crossings
Meet oncoming Traffic
Blind & Open Junctions
General Driving Information
Show Me Tell Me
Taking Your Theory Test
Taking Your Practical Test

This book is a self-study book that once read will help prepare you for your practical driving test. It will enable you to proceed through your training more rapidly and it should reduce the amount of time needed with an ADI (If you require one) There are step-by-step exercises to run through and routines at the end of each exercise that will help you to remember what to do.

There are colour photos and diagrams that show where to position the car when practising. Take each exercise that you are dealing with and study it carefully.

If you do not use an ADI and wish to be taught by an experienced driver, they must be 21 years of age and have held a licence for 3 years or more.

The person being taught to drive must be able to read a vehicle number plate from roughly about 20 metres or 66 feet, if glasses are needed to do this then you must wear them for driving. The practice car must be insured for you to use and have L-Plates clearly displayed on the car while practising. If you are unsure, about taking a trainee on to the open road, then please contact a qualified driving Instructor.

Buy a second interior mirror that comes with a suction pad (these are available at most car parts suppliers for a few pounds) and place it next to the interior mirror so that the experienced driver can keep an eye on what is happening from behind.

Remember this:

AN ALERT DRIVER IS A SAFE DRIVER

Here are a few examples of the Photo's & Diagrams that are in the book.

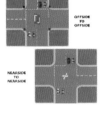

Table of Contents

Abbreviations

It is <u>VERY</u> important that we learn what is on this page, especially <u>POM</u>.

<u>DSSSM:</u> <u>is used for setting yourself up in a car that someone else has driven.</u>

<u>Door.</u> Make sure your door is firmly closed.

<u>Seat.</u> Move up or down – forward or back.

<u>Steering.</u> Arms should have slight bend at the elbow, adjust back of seat forward or back.

<u>Seatbelt.</u> Make sure seat belt has no kinks in it.

<u>Mirrors.</u> Adjust interior mirror with left hand and with your head looking straight in front.

<u>POM:</u> <u>is used when ready to first move off, away from the kerb.</u>

<u>Prepare.</u> Clutch down, into 1st, Up to Biting Point, Cover Gas, Feet still.

<u>Observation.</u> **Six** points starting over your left shoulder, looking out of the rear side window.

<u>Move.</u> Set the Gas, Handbrake off and then final check over your right shoulder as you go.

<u>MSM:</u> <u>is used when you first move off or alter your course.</u>

<u>Mirrors.</u> Interior first followed by either the left or right for turn or manoeuvre.

Signal. Indicate either left or right, remember to cancel signal once manoeuvre is complete.

Manoeuvre. Move off, turn left or right, or move over to another lane.

LADA: is used if you stopped at a T-Junction or about to turn Right.

Look. Look to see if it is clear to emerge or turn right.

Assess. Assess the situation; identify a gap in the traffic where you can safely turn.

Decide. Decide what is the correct safe gap in the on-coming traffic.

Act. When you have identified your gap check left and right again and then go.

Exercise 1: Cockpit Drill & Controls

The objective of this exercise is to be able to identify and operate the main car controls.

I would be useful to either go to a quite car park or use your own driveway, and have the trainee run through the gears and get used to the clutch, etc.

Note: When you start any of these exercises, please turn off your mobile phone if you have one.

The cockpit drill & controls consists of the following:

Doors.
Seat, Inc Headrest.
Steering.
Seatbelt.
Mirrors.

Doors:
Make sure your door is closed firmly, before opening the door, check your door mirror for any passing traffic, bikes etc.

Seat & Head Restraint:

The seat will move forward/backwards and up and down to allow you to find the correct position for driving. Make sure that you head restraint is level with your head in case of an impact from behind.

Steering:
Place your hands on the wheel, check that your arms have a slight bend at the elbow. Adjusting the back of your seat may be necessary in order to achieve this.

Seatbelt:
Put on your seatbelt and make sure there are no twists in it; this would be viewed as a **minor fault.**

Mirrors:
There are three mirrors on your car, an interior mirror and two door mirrors. Adjust the interior mirror (See Picture 1) so that you can see the entire back window in it.

(Picture 1) You should be able to see out the back window through the interior mirror.

Adjust each door mirror so that when you turn your head to look at it you should see only about the thickness of a thumb of the side of your car and an equal half of the road and sky. (See Picture 2)

(Picture 2) What you should be able to see through your left/right door mirrors.

Foot Controls

There are three foot pedals, these make the car move, stop and be able to change gear. This section deals with the following:

Accelerator. (Gas)
Brake (Footbrake)
Clutch. (Biting Point & Stalling)

A way to help you remember each pedal is: From right to left, remember them as '**ABC**'

Accelerator:
The accelerator is quite light, but is very sensitive and even the slightest pressure on it will propel the car forward, especially in lower gears.

Brake (Foot Brake):
Press the footbrake and you will see that it feels a lot harder than the gas pedal. This must be pressed gently and progressively'.

Clutch:
Each time you require to change gear, you must depress the clutch and change gear accordingly.

Biting Point & Stalling:
When you select first gear in order to move off you must bring the clutch up slowly, you will

start to feel the car shudder slightly, and this is known as the **Biting Point**.

Note: You will soon find out how important it is to keep your left leg still (at Biting Point) when you are about to move off, I call the left leg the 'Governor' because it governs whether or not you drive off smoothly or stall.

Hand Controls

This section deals with the following:

Hand brake
Gears
Indicators
Zone of Vision: Including Mirrors
Other Minor Controls

Hand brake (Parking Brake):
The hand brake is there to secure the car when stationary or if you have stopped momentarily on a hill

Gears:
Neutral is when the gear stick has not been placed in any gear at all. The first gear is your power gear; to get the car moving. The second & third gears are your working gears and these are mainly for getting you around town i.e. turning corners and at roundabouts etc. the fourth gear is for normal driving and the fifth gear is for dual carriageways or motorway driving.

Indicators:
The indicators are usually located on the left or right of the steering wheel. Identify where they are.

Zone of Vision: Including Mirrors

Forward Zone:
Your forward zone is what you can see directly through your front window.

Peripheral Vision:
Your peripheral vision is what you can see to your left and right even though you are looking straight ahead.

Interior Mirror:
The interior mirror looks out of the rear window and gives you a view of what is directly behind you.

Door Mirrors:
Both the left and right door mirrors show you what is either side of the vehicle and they are both convex (slightly bevelled) in shape. This allows for a wider field of vision.

Other Controls:
Your experienced driver will take you through the other controls that need to be explained to you, these include:

Window wipers.
Hazard warning switch.
Headlights/Sidelights.
Front & rear fog lights.
How to de-mist the front and back windows.

<u>**You have now completed Exercise 1.**</u>

<u>**Exercise 2: Moving Off & Stopping**</u>

The objective of this exercise is to be able to start the car, move off safely, drive alone the road a short distance and pull up in a safe and convenient place on the left.

Note: Make sure that the road you chose for this exercise is as long and straight as possible; this will enable you to repeat moving off and stopping a number of times.

<u>This section deals with the following:</u>

Precautions before starting the car
POM
MSM
Securing the car
Recovering the car (After stalling)
Parking point

<u>**Precautions before starting the car:**</u>

Ensure the handbrake is up fully, the car is in neutral & start the car.

<u>**POM: Prepare, Observe and Move.**</u>

Prepare:
To prepare the car do the following:

To **'Set the Gas'** apply a little pressure on the gas pedal; Try this before you start your POM so as to get the feel of it.

Clutch down, select first Gear, set The Gas, bring the clutch up to biting point, and keep your feet still.

Observations:
Start with a quick look over your left shoulder, checking door mirrors and the interior, finishing over your right shoulder.

Move:
You are now in a position to move off, assuming that it is safe to do so.

MSM: Mirror, Signal, And Manoeuvre.
MSM is the procedure that you will use for pulling up and stopping safely on the left, and also before you steer the car in any direction.

Securing The Car:
When you have pulled up near the kerb you will have to secure the car, this is done by:

Hand brake on, in to neutral, feet off the pedals, cancel the signal.

Recovering The Car:

If you stall the car then do the following:

1. Keep both feet firmly down on clutch & brake, into 1st Gear, start Car, biting point, foot off brake. (When safe to do so)

Parking Point:

A parking point is what you use to park the car near to the kerb without damaging your tyres or wheels. To find your parking point, park close to the kerb and look through the front window. Where you see the kerb intercept the window wiper or a point on the dashboard, (See Picture 1) this is your parking point, remember where it is. When you intend to pull up and park, you will notice your parking point getting closer to the kerb. Make sure the kerb does not go past your parking point or you will hit it.

Picture 1. Kerb in relations to window wiper.

You have now completed Exercise 2.

Exercise 3: Approach Junctions to Turn Left

The objective of Exercise 3 & 4 is to be able to approach junctions and turn left. In order to do this, we first need to know the difference between turning left and emerging left, (Emerging left is discussed in a later exercise) If I asked you to turn into the next road on the left, then you will be turning from a Major road (that you are on) into a Minor road. Emerging left is when you come to the end of a road and wish to turn left/right i.e. at a T-Junction. This is known as Minor to Major.

This section deals with the following:

Approach Junctions to Turn Left
Coasting
Engine Braking
Major to Minor
Minor to Major

Imagine driving along a road and you wish to take the next road on the left, at this point you would use the routine to turn left (see below) You have right of way (assuming it is clear to turn) and will cross over a single broken white line into that road, this is what we refer to as turning left. It is also known as turning **Major to Minor**. This is because you are on a Major road and wish to turn in to a Minor road. (See Diagram 1)

Diagram 1   **TURN LEFT**

Emerging left is when you come to the end of a road and wish to turn left i.e. at a T-Junction or Crossroads, so you will have to stop at the double broken white lines before emerging. This also applies to turning right and emerging right, which are a bit harder to do, as you will find out in Exercises 4 & 6.

Routine To Turn Left:

As I stated earlier, each part of driving has a routine that must be followed. I have broken down what is meant by each one on the right hand side so that you may understand what you are doing. Take a look at Exercise 13 Virtual Driving to see how useful each routine is.

The routine for 'Turning Left'

Interior

Check interior for what is behind you.

Left

Check left mirror for bikes etc.

Indicate

Give your intention of turning left.

Position

Make sure that you are about 1 Metre from the kerb.

Brake (Gently)

Slow the car down to an appropriate speed.

Clutch Down

Clutch down before you get to the corner.

Second Gear

Select second gear.

Clutch Up

Slowly allow for engine braking for the ideal speed to turn.

Follow Corner Round

This will keep you in your lane.

Gas

Apply a little gas.

Check Mirror

See who may be following you round.

Note: As you approach to turn left, look out for sharp corners and pedestrians that may have started crossing.

Study this routine above carefully (just the words in BOLD) and memories them. The better you can repeat them back, the easier it will be. If you can print each routine off, it will be easier to study. Ask someone to check each step to see how you are doing. When you can repeat it back in the correct sequence then you are ready to try it out in the car.

If you are studying this exercise in the home, then try to imagine that you are in a car driving along a road and about to turn left, run through the routine in your mind. I call this 'Virtual Driving' (See Exercise 13 for Virtual Driving) you can go through it time and time again until you are happy that you know it of-by-heart.

In the routine, I make it clear that the clutch goes down, you then select second gear and then clutch comes up. It is very important that the clutch is brought up before turning otherwise the car will be **'Coasting'** This means there will be no **'Engine Braking'** to help slow the car down.

When you bring the clutch up slowly until we hear and feel the car at biting point, this helps to slow the car down and achieve the ideal speed to turn left. If you were to leave the clutch down after selecting second then the car will be moving faster as you turn left, making you brake harder in order to slow down to a safe speed for turning.

<u>You have now completed Exercise 3.</u>

Exercise 4: Approach Junctions to Turn Right

How to Turn Right-To-Go **(No Oncoming Traffic)**

Turning right is a little bit harder, due to having to cross oncoming traffic. I have broken this routine into two similar, but different routines. These are known as:

Right to Go & Right to Stop

Just because there is no oncoming traffic make sure before you turn right that look into the new road, and look out for sharp corners, parked cars and pedestrians who may have started crossing. (Keep alert)

Your point of turn, is when your right door mirror is just before the middle centre line in the new road, (See Diagram 1) this should also stop you 'cutting the corner' in the new road. Cutting the corner means that you turned into the new road too early, cutting over the emerging lane of that road, you could impact a vehicle waiting to emerge from that road.

(See Diagram 1)

Diagram 1

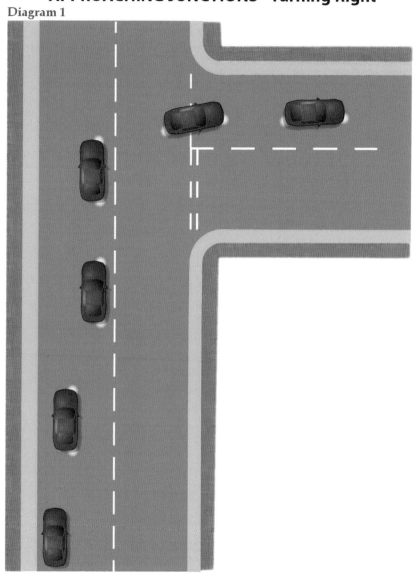

The routine for turning 'Right to go' (No Oncoming Traffic)

Interior

Check interior for what is behind you.

Right

Check right mirror for bikes etc.

Indicate

Give your intention of turning right.

Position

Make sure you are to the left of the centre line in the middle of road.

Brake (Gently)

Slow the car down to an appropriate speed.

Clutch Down

Clutch down before you get to the corner.

Second Gear

Select second gear.

Clutch Up

Slowly allow for engine braking for the ideal speed to turn.

Follow Line Round

This will keep you to your lane.

Gas

Apply a little gas.

Check Mirror

See who has followed you round.

How to Turn Right-To-Stop **(Oncoming Traffic)**

The routine to 'turn right to stop' is that little bit more difficult than the previous two, this is because there will be oncoming traffic that will require you to stop. When you have stopped you will use a routine called **'LADA'** this stands for Look, Assess, Decide and Act. (See Abbreviations) You will find that you use LADA a great number of times in driving.

Your point of stop, is when your right door mirror is just before the middle centre line in the new road, this should also stop you 'cutting the corner' in the new road. Look out for sharp corners, parked cars and pedestrians that may start to cross as you start to turn. (Keep alert as you wait for a clearing to turn)

Remember: <u>Do not cut the corner.</u>

APPROACHING JUNCTIONS - Turning Right

Diagram 1

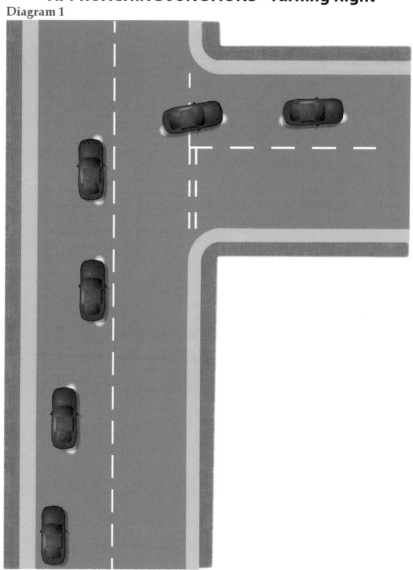

The routine for turning 'Right to Stop' (Oncoming Traffic)

Interior

Check interior for what is behind you.

Right

Check right mirror for bikes etc.

Indicate

Give your intention of turning right.

Position

Make sure you are the left of centre line in the middle of road.

Brake to Stop

Right mirror just before middle centre line in the new road.

Clutch Down (Before Stop)

Clutch down before you get to the corner.

Into First, Biting Point, Foot On Brake

Keep clutch at biting point, do not stall.

L.A.D.A.

Go when safe to do so.

Follow Line Round

This will keep you in your lane.

Gas

Apply a little gas.

Check Mirror

See who has followed you round.

<u>**You have now completed Exercise 4.**</u>

<u>**Exercise 5: Blind & Open Junctions**</u>

Before we move on to T-Junctions Emerge Right/Left I would like to cover these points.

Blind Junction
Open Junction
Stop Sign
Peep and Creep
The Walking Rule

A **Blind Junction** is when you are approaching the end of a road and you cannot see clearly in to the new road; your vision may be blocked due to walls, buildings, trees etc. This type of junction is known as a 'Blind' junction. It will be very difficult to see what is in the new road until you get to the end of your road. (See Peep and Creep)

An **Open Junction** is when you can see clearly into the new road before you reach the junction, for example, a field either side of you would allow you to see clearly to one or both sides. In this situation you could see if there were any cars approaching from your right or not, if it was clear, you could select second gear and turn without stopping.

Note 1: Be careful with this until you are confident and can guess distances of other cars approaching. (See the Walking Rule)

Note 2: When you see a **STOP** sign, you must stop at this sign, the double broken line will be replaced with one continuous line; do not cross over it without first coming to a <u>complete stop</u>.

<u>Peep And Creep:</u>

Peep and Creep is used when you are at a blind junction and there may be vehicles close to the left and right of you blocking your view. When you want to move off and you cannot see clearly, use Peep and Creep; this allows you to move forward a little at a time until you have a clearer view of the oncoming traffic.

With the car at biting point and your foot on the foot brake, keep your left foot still and up at biting point, <u>lightly</u> lift you foot off the brake momentarily and back on again, each time you do this the car moves forward, turn the steering wheel slightly in the direction that you are turning each time you move forward.

To improve your line of sight you may have to lean forward to the steering wheel as much as you need to, and as the car moves forward you view should start to improve, do this as many times as required until it is safe to go.

The Walking Rule:

Assuming you are waiting to turn right, if you are unsure if the gap between the vehicles coming towards is big enough for you to proceed, then you can use 'The Walking Rule' What I mean by this is; imagine yourself walking briskly across the road in that gap, if you can, then this would be a good enough gap for you to proceed with the turn.

Note: If you have time to walk across the road, you have time to drive across the road.

You have now completed Exercise 5.

Exercise 6: T–Junctions, Emerge Left

This exercise is on how to emerge left at a T-junction, this is different from turning left, because instead of turning left from a major road to a minor road, you will be going from a minor road on to a major road i.e. when you come to the end of a road.

Again look at the diagram and take time to explain what Major to Minor & Minor to Major roads are to the trainee, so that they know that they have to give way on emerging.

(See Diagram 1)

Diagram 1

T-JUNCTION, EMERGING

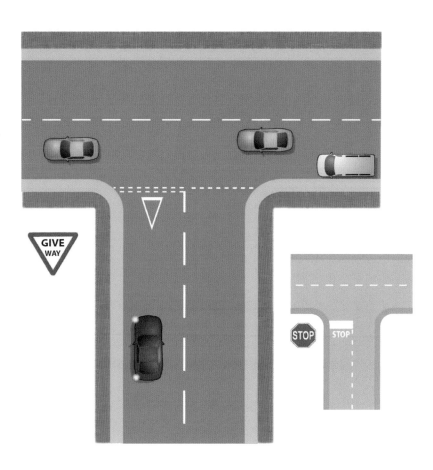

You will see a 'Give Way' sign and a triangle in the middle of your lane as you approach the end of your road, and then double broken white lines. When we approach these lines, slow the car down gently as you get nearer them, do not change down gears, remember you are going to this junction with every intention of stopping (See Blind & Open Junctions)

There are nearly always five white lines in the middle of the road as you come to emerge. As you are slowing down and as you reach the white lines, start to count down from 5,4,3 and when you get to the second white line, put the clutch down and select first gear. So as you approach the end of the road the routine you should apply for this is '5,4,3,2 into 1' leave the clutch down and look right, left and right.

If it is clear and safe to go then bring the clutch up slowly and turn left. If, when you look and there are oncoming cars then stop. Just before you stop turn the steering wheel ½ or 1 full turn left, depending on the shape of the corner, this will help when you to turn in to the new road and not swing out too much into oncoming traffic. Now use 'LADA' to help you emerge safely.

You have now completed Exercise 6.

The routine for Emerging Left

Interior

Check interior for what is behind you.

Left

Check left mirror for bikes etc.

Indicate

Give your intention of turning left.

Position

Make sure that you are about 1 Metre from the kerb.

Brake to Stop

Double broken lines disappear under the bonnet.

Clutch Down Before Stop

Check broken white line under door mirror.

Into First, Biting Point, Foot On Brake

Keep clutch at biting point, do not stall.

L.A.D.A.

Go when safe to do so.

Follow Kerb Round

This will keep you in your lane.

Gas

Move through the gears up to the appropriate speed limit.

Check Mirror

See who is behind you in the new road.

Exercise 7: T-Junctions – Emerge Right

This exercise is on how to emerge right at a T-junction, this exercise is very similar to exercise 6, so make sure you have covered that exercise before continuing with this one.

To emerge right is a lot more difficult than to emerge left. This is because you have to cross oncoming traffic and also join traffic on the other side.

You will see a **'Give Way'** sign and a triangle in the middle of your lane as you approach the end of your road, and then double broken white lines. When we approach these lines, slow the car down gently as you get nearer them, do not change down gears, remember you are going to this junction with every intention of stopping (See Blind & Open Junctions) (See Diagram 1)

Diagram 1

T-JUNCTION, EMERGING

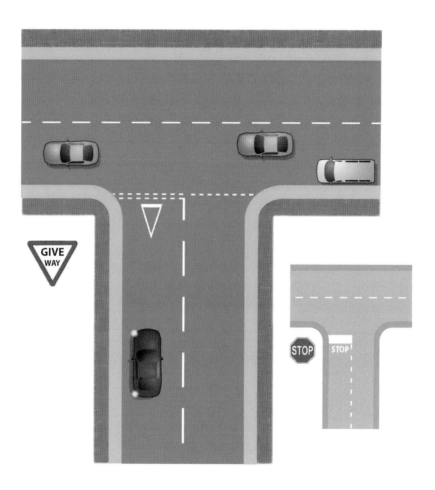

There are nearly always five white lines in the middle of the road as you come to emerge. As you are slowing down and as you reach the white lines, start to count down from 5,4,3 and when you get to the second white line, put the clutch down and select 1st gear. So as you approach the end of the road the routine you should apply for this is '5,4,3,2 into 1' leave the clutch down and look right, left and right.

On emerging right, keep the position of the car close to the middle white line in your road. When you stop, look right, then left, then right again and if it is clear and safe to go, bring the clutch up slowly and turn right into your lane. If, there are oncoming cars then stop. Keep the steering wheel straight and the position of the car straight in relation to the middle line in your road. Now use 'LADA' to help you emerge safely.

If the road on your right is clear and there are vehicles in the lane to your left that you are about to join, do not move out and sit in the middle of the road, as you may block any traffic to your right while waiting for the road to clear. You may have to be there for some time until the opposite road clears, so hold back and keep alert.

You have now completed Exercise 7.

The routine to Emerge Right

Interior

Check interior for what is behind you.

Left

Check left mirror for bikes etc.

Indicate

Give your intention of turning left.

Position

Just to left of the centre white line.

Brake to Stop

Double broken lines disappear under the bonnet.

Clutch Down Before Stop

Check single broken white line under door mirror.

Into First, Biting Point, Foot On Brake

Keep clutch at biting point, do not stall.

L.A.D.A.

Go when safe to do so.

Move across into lane

Move into lane.

Gas

Move through the gears up to the appropriate speed limit.

Check Mirror

See who is behind you in the new road.

Exercise 8: Traffic Lights (Uncontrolled/Controlled Crossroads)

There are two types of crossroads to deal with; **No Traffic lights** (uncontrolled crossroads) and **Traffic lights** (controlled crossroads) these crossroads may also be staggered i.e. with the road ahead of you slightly offset.

A crossroads is very similar to emerging at a T-junction, really it is a T-Junction but with an extra road ahead of it. You should see a 'Crossroads Sign' as you approach. So follow the routines in Exercises 6 & 7 depending on which way you want to turn or go straight ahead over the crossing. That is basically it apart from how you deal with vehicles in the road ahead of you.

Assuming that you wish to turn right, then you would use the routine in exercise 7 'T-Junctions – Emerge Right' When you come to a stop, you will use 'LADA' to help you emerge into the new road or cross over both lanes. You should look to your right then straight ahead then to your left then back to straight ahead of you and then to your right and so until you are sure it is safe to go.

Note: See Blind & Open Junctions and also Peep & Creep.

(See Diagram 1)

Diagram 1   **CROSSROADS**

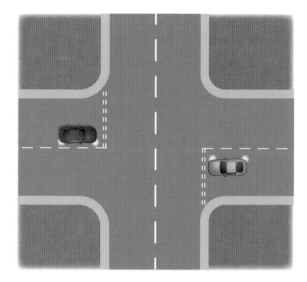

**STAGGERED
CROSSROADS**

Assuming that you have followed the Exercise 7 and you are now stopped at the double white lines and you are in first gear, biting point and foot firmly on foot brake, then do the following:

Look Right
Look Ahead
Look Left
Look Ahead
Look Right

When safe to proceed then do so, keeping an eye on any vehicles opposite you as you move off.

In this scenario, imagine wanting to turn right, and there are no vehicles coming from your right hand lane, there is a vehicle in front of you with no directional indicators on, and the body position of the car is straight, so we can assume that it wants to go straight over at the junction. At this point, you should always ask the question, is it really going that way? Some drivers don't bother to indicate at junctions and this is how a lot of accidents occur. They will have right of way over you if you are turning right and crossing in front of their path, so give way to them.

If they were to flash their headlights allowing you to proceed in front of them (as does happen some times) then before you start to turn, make sure you re-check if it is still safe to proceed as the road condition may have changed. Proceed with caution in case they hadn't meant to flash you.

Traffic Lights (Controlled Crossroads)

Light controlled crossings are slightly easier as you are controlled by the traffic lights. For going straight over at the crossing, always take your left hand lane unless it is for left turn only (remember to check your left mirror if you have to move into that lane as you approach) (See Diagram 2)

LIGHT CONTROLLED CROSSROADS

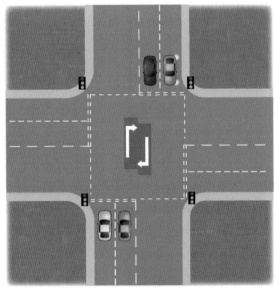

**OFFSIDE
TO
OFFSIDE**

**NEARSIDE
TO
NEARSIDE**

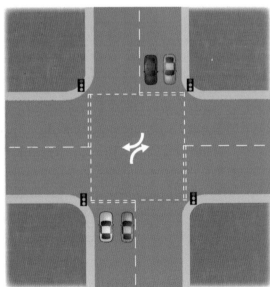

If the lights are red, then stop, apply the handbrake, select neutral and cover the clutch and gas pedals, do not sit there at biting point as it could be some time before the lights change, this will only wear out your clutch. If you are the first vehicle at the lights, then look for information as to when to prepare the car to go, i.e. cars going through the lights, slowing down and stopping.

For turning right, make sure you pass any roads on your right before you signal, as a there could be a vehicle wanting to pull out of that road and may think you want to turn before the lights, it could pull out in front of you. Take up position to move across to that lane and check your right mirror before you move, if the lights are red, apply the handbrake, select neutral and cover the clutch and gas pedals.

There is no rush to turn right at traffic lights, when the lights turn to green, and you are the first or second vehicle, you will move slowly forward and take up position in the middle of the junction waiting for a safe gap to cross (Generally two vehicles will move into the junction on turning right) if you find that you are the third vehicle then move forward as the other two take up position to turn and stop at the line to access the junction. (A bus equals two vehicles) If one or both vehicles proceed through the junction and assuming your light is still on green, you will move forward and take up position to turn.

At some junctions there is a 4th light under the green light, this is known as a filter lane light and has a green arrow pointing right, when this light illuminates it allows a number of cars to proceed through the crossing at that time.

There may be road markings in the middle of the junction that will inform you how to turn right, i.e. any cars approaching you, wishing to turn to their right may have to cross either in front of you or behind you. This is known as **'Nearside to Nearside,** or **'Offside to Offside'**, there may be arrows in the middle of the junction or boxes that you move into that you have to follow in order to turn safely.

If there are no road markings the to turn, then turning will be determined by the shape of a junction and the actions of other drivers ahead of you.

Note: Nearside is the left side of the car that is closest to the kerb when parked up on the left of the road. Offside is the driver's side of the car.

<u>**You have now completed Exercise 8.**</u>

Exercise 9: Roundabouts

Roundabouts seem to be every trainee's nightmare; there can be a lot happening very quickly, so it's best to understand how you are going to deal with them in your mind prior to dealing with one for real.

There are a number of roundabouts to deal with; mini roundabouts, roundabouts with three or four roads joining them and the big gyratory system that have two or three lanes around them and five or more roads joining them, the gyratory system are mostly light controlled so their not as big and bad as they sound.

When you encounter a roundabout, <u>you must approach it with every intention of going there to stop.</u> I suggest that you approach it at the same speed that you would approach a blind T-Junction i.e. <u>slowly</u>. (See Diagram 1)

Diagram 1 **ROUNDABOUTS**

In this example we will deal with a roundabout with four lanes. Assuming that you wanted to turn right, then this would be the third exit; you would use MSM to move over to the right hand lane.

As you get closer to the roundabout you should have quick look to your right and ahead of you, but also be checking your own lane position as you approach, lane discipline is very important as it can be quite easy to accidentally wander into another lane; quick observations are needed here. If the road on your right is clear, then glance to the lane ahead of you, if this is also clear then you may select first or second and go, the gear you select will depend on the speed that the car is moving when you decide to go.

As you enter the roundabout, be aware that some one might pull out in front of you on the left. Keep close to the middle of the roundabout as you go round it (keep to the left hand lane for going straight on) to leave the roundabout at your exit you should indicate as you pass the exit prior to the one you want to leave, checking your left mirror as you do so.

Note: For exiting a Mini roundabout you do not have to indicate when you leave it, as they are small and there may be no time to do this.

You have now completed Exercise 9.

Exercise 10: Pedestrian Crossings

There are controlled and uncontrolled pedestrian crossings, you need to be aware of them all; this is why you should have passed or at least started your Theory test. I'm sure as a pedestrian you have used all of them at some point. Now as a driver you will have to deal with them from a driver's point of view.

Approach a light controlled Pedestrian Crossing That's Clear:

MSM (On approach)
Is it clear?
Check interior mirror
Will it be clear when I get there?
Ease off gas
Clear on both sides?
Then proceed through

Uncontrolled Crossing (Zebra):

An uncontrolled crossing is known as a Zebra crossing, this is uncontrolled because there is nothing to make a driver stop when someone wants to cross; it is down to the driver to stop. So be **alert** as you approach one **and be ready to stop**.

A zebra crossing has black & white strips across the road, black & white poles either side of it, with flashing amber lights and Zigzag lines either side of it, do not overtake or park on these lines, not even to drop someone off.

When you approach a crossing you should use the routine MSM (Mirror, Signal, Manoeuvre) Check your interior mirror and if a vehicle is very close behind you then start to reduce your speed, even though the crossing is clear ahead of you, it can change very quickly and you may have to brake accordingly.

Watch out for Brake lights ahead at a crossing and start to slow down, if you stop, make sure that you apply the handbrake if people are still on the crossing or about to cross. If a car was to hit your car from behind, then with the handbrake on it could prevent you being pushed into the people on the crossing.

If a crossing has an island in the middle (double crossing) then we must treat this as one crossing. If your side of the crossing is clear and someone is about to step on the other crossing, then you can go, if safe to do so. But if a person is halfway over the other crossing walking towards you then you must stop for them. Never wave pedestrians across, as this may distract them from traffic coming from the other direction.

I want you to ask yourself these two questions when you approach a crossing:

Is it clear?
Will it be clear when I get there?

It's very important that you ask yourself these questions as it could be up to 5 - 10 seconds or more before you get close to it. You will find that when approaching a crossing, people can step onto it at the last minute without looking, keep alert until you are through it.

Light Controlled Crossings:

Approach a light controlled Pedestrian Crossing that's Not Clear:

MSM (On approach)
Is it clear?
Will it be clear when I get there?
Check interior mirror
Ease off gas
Pedestrians approaching
Brake to stop, clutch down before stop
Handbrake on (If there are a lot of people crossing)
First gear, biting point, cover gas
Clear on both sides?
Then proceed through

There are four types of light controlled crossings that have traffic lights, these are:

Pelican
Puffin
Toucan
Pegasus

Pelican Crossing:
As a pedestrian you will probably have used this one the most, this is the one with the flashing person and the continuous bleeping noise that you hear when you should not start to cross but continue to cross if you are already on the crossing. As a driver, you will see the red stop light change to flashing amber, at this point it will only be safe to go if the crossing is clear, do not go if there are people still on the crossing.

Puffin Crossing:
A Puffin crossing has no flashing amber sequence, instead it has a sensor on each light looking down at the crossing, when someone starts to cross it will sense they are there and keep the lights at red until the crossing is clear. When it senses there is no one on the crossing it will change the traffic lights to amber then green. (No flashing amber)

Toucan Crossing:

A Toucan crossing allows Pedestrians and Bicycles to cross at the same time, this is why it is called a toucan, two can cross at once. You can probably guess that you are driving up to a toucan crossing as there will be a bicycle lane running up to it. It also has a normal traffic light sequence as the puffin does.

Pegasus Crossing:
There is also a Pegasus crossing; these are for people on horseback. The button that they press to stop traffic is quite high up; this is so the person on the horse doesn't have to dismount in order to use it.

You have now completed Exercise 10.

Exercise 11: Meeting Oncoming Vehicles

This exercise deals with meeting oncoming vehicles as you drive along the road and how you deal with them safely. This section deals with the following:

Tunnels
Stepping Out
Priority
Holding Position
Relief Area

As you drive along a road you will inevitably meet other vehicles coming in the opposite direction. This should be no problem as long as the vehicle approaching you stays in its own lane and does not cross over the centre line of the road. If it does, it is **'Stepping Out'** as there may be an obstruction ahead of it forcing it to do so, maybe a parked car, road-works etc that will make the oncoming vehicle move out of its lane and into yours. Sometimes this is fine as the width of the road may allow for this.

If your lane is clear of any obstructions, and you notice an oncoming vehicle stepping out, it may cause you to take avoiding action. The road may be wide enough for it to do so, but be aware of it until it is safely past. You will also find that there are obstructions in your lane that you will have to deal with, how do you deal with them safely?

Imagine driving along a road and there is a parked vehicle in your lane and you need to avoid it. You have to ask the question: can I safely pass the parked vehicle or should I hold back or slow down to allow on-coming traffic past first. Who has **Priority?** Is it safe to step out? Can both my car and the approaching vehicles pass safely? Should I slow down or maybe stop and assume the holding position? These are questions that all drivers should ask when they get a situation like this one. If you are in any doubt whatsoever then start to slow down and stop if need be.

Note1: Never accelerate towards on oncoming vehicle with a parked vehicle either side of you. You never know how much the on-coming vehicle will step out and you are accelerating towards them.

Note2: Before you step out you must check your interior then right mirrors, then after you have passed the obstruction, you should check your left door mirror before moving back into your lane.

If you do stop, then you will be in what is known as a **'Holding Position'** this holding position is roughly (where possible) 1½ to 2 car lengths from the car in front and not too near the kerb so as to not make someone behind you think that you have parked up. When you assume a hold back position, make sure you leave enough room for the oncoming vehicle to pass you safely. After the vehicle has passed, and it's safe to go, then you <u>must</u> check your right door mirror before moving. A cyclist or motorbike could have pulled up either side of you as you were waiting to go.

Two vehicles parked opposite each other on each side of the road are what is called a **'Tunnel'** It's very important to ask all the questions stated earlier, who has priority? Can both of us pass safely? Etc. If you are closer to the tunnel than the oncoming vehicle, and it is safe to go, then check your mirrors and step out into the tunnel. Remember this: **<u>If in doubt, cut it out</u>**, if you are unsure then start to give way to it.

When the road is narrow, full observations and anticipation are required until you have passed safely. Main roads are usually wide enough to allow safe passing of vehicles in both directions and also allow for parked vehicles. Some town centre roads are quite tight; so reduce your speed for the width of the road. Side roads are where you will find most tunnels. If the road has many vehicles parked in it there will be a lot of tunnels for you to deal with as you drive along.

There will also be a lot of **'Relief Areas'** these are areas that do not have any vehicles parked, or access to houses, etc. As you drive alone a road like this, there may be many occasions when you will have to stop, slow down or adopt the holding position, so be alert and always ask questions.

As you drive down a narrow road and you see a parked vehicle with its brake lights on, ask yourself: have they just pulled up and parked? They might open the car door or suddenly want to pull out, either way, be aware that this could be a problem. Also be aware of pedestrians wanting to cross between parked cars and cyclists.

As you drive along, I want you to recognise when you are in a Tunnel environment and ask yourself, any or all of these questions in order to deal safely with the problem:

Who has priority?
Should I slowdown or go?
Is it safe to go?
Can both vehicles pass safely?
If I stop, where should I stop?

<u>You have now completed Exercise 11.</u>

Exercise 12: General Driving Information

This exercise deals with general driving information as you drive along the road, you will encounter many different situations as you go, always ask questions of what is happening in front of you and how are you going to deal with it. Remember: An alert driver is a safe driver.

This section and also covers:

One metre boundary
2-second rule
3 things to do on a straight road
Adverse conditions
Blocking roads
Buses
Bus lanes
Chevron
Pedestrian refuge
Cyclists
Dead ground
Dual carriageways
Overtaking
T & T (Tyres on Tarmac)

One metre boundary

Imagine a One metre boundary all-round the car and try to keep all obstacles clear of you, the closer you get to objects the slower the car should be.

2 Second rule

The 2-second rule will help you to keep the correct distance from the vehicle in front as you drive. To check if you are too close, when the vehicle in front of you passes a stationary object like a parked car or streetlight etc. then count 2 seconds and if you pass that object before you finish counting then you are too close to it.

Remember this: **Only a fool breaks the 2-second rule.**

For wet conditions the rule will change to 4 seconds and for icy conditions 10 seconds. Remember that when you start counting, start with the word, Go, as the vehicle passes the stationary object, then 1 2 etc.

3 Things to do on a straight road

When you are driving on a long stretch of straight road there are 3 things you can do. Check your interior mirror, your position in the road and your speed for that particular road. **(Interior, position, speed)** Do not do this if you are driving round a bend or dealing with an obstacle in front of you, they will require your full attention.

Adverse conditions

What do we mean by adverse conditions; well it really applies to a number of weather conditions:

rain, heavy rain, fog, snow, ice and wind. When driving in any of these conditions you must be more alert as you vision may be impaired and the car can react differently. Put you lights on when conditions worsen and your fog lights in fog, remember to switch them off if conditions improve. Remember the 2-second rule and adjust accordingly for each condition. Be aware that fallen leaves in autumn may also cause the car to skid, so drive slower in these conditions, especially round bends.

Blocking roads

When moving slowly in heavy traffic remember that if you have to stop, always make sure you do not block the access to a road to your left, it may be some time before you move on and if a vehicle wants to turn into that road, and cant because of you, then they might be blocking the cars behind them, all because of where you stopped.

Buses

Buses are forever stopping to drop off and pick up passengers, so when you are behind a bus, or for that matter any large vehicle, always leave more distance than you would with a car, this will allow a better view up front, and allow you time to overtake it safely if you need to. Watch out for pedestrians crossing as they leave the bus and any buses pulling out quickly without signalling.

Bus lanes
When you see a bus lane ahead of you and you are driving in the inside lane, look for information as to what times, (if any) you are allowed to use that lane. If there are restrictions, and you cannot use it at this time, then move out into the next lane, remember there may be cameras watching that lane, don't take a chance.

Chevron
A chevron is a black sign with white arrows pointing to the left or right, when you are driving along a road and you see one ahead of you, it is a warning that there is a sharp bend ahead, either to the left or right, slow down as you may have no idea just how sharp it is. They may also be on some roundabouts.

Pedestrian refuge
A pedestrian refuge is a little island in the middle of the road; it may have yellow bollards either side of it. Pedestrians can cross halfway in a road and wait for the other half of the road to clear. Pedestrians do not have right of way so if you see someone crossing into one, expect them to wait if you are approaching them, but do not treat it like a Zebra crossing and stop for them. Keep an eye on them in case they step out in front of you.

Cyclists

When you encounter a cyclist always pass them carefully, they may swing out in front of you car to avoid something in the road. You must, where possible, give a cyclist a 2-metre clearance as you pass them. This is because the bike is 1 metre high and the cyclist sitting on top of it is also roughly 1 metre. If they were to fall over in front of you then there is a better chance of avoiding them. Never overtake a cyclist on a pedestrian crossing or at pedestrian refuge.

Dead ground

When you drive up a hill, you will not be able to see what is over the top of it; this is what we call dead ground. You must slow down slightly just before you get to the top as there could be a someone crossing the road or there could be vehicles backed up etc. don't leave it too late and be caught out.

Dual carriageways

When you drive on a dual carriageway always remember to stay in the left lane unless you have to overtake a vehicle. If you have to overtake then remember to check your mirrors, signal early and take a quick glance to your right before slowly moving into the next lane. Move back into the left lane when you are clear to do so. If you are driving on a dual carriageway with three lanes, do not stay in the middle lane even though you are up to the correct speed for that road.

Overtaking

If you are about to overtake a vehicle, ask yourself these questions: Is safe it, Is it necessary and is it legal, **(Safe, Necessary, Legal)** never overtake on a bend, a hill, a pedestrian crossing or anywhere else where you think it could be dangerous.

T & T (Tyres on Tarmac)

Whenever you stop in a queue of traffic always make sure you can see 'tyres on tarmac' do not get too close to the vehicle in front, stop so that you can see their tyres on the tarmac, this will help if the vehicle in front of you was to brake down, allowing you room to manoeuvre around it. If you are too close you may also have exhaust fumes coming into your car. Remember T&T even in slow moving traffic.

You have now completed Exercise 12.

Exercise 13: Virtual Driving

Virtual driving is something that I devised to help you run through your routines in your mind. Once you can repeat back each of the routines flawlessly then its time to go for a Virtual Drive. If you know what to do before you set out, the easier it should be when you start to apply these routines in the car.

The main areas to concentrate on are the three **routines** for turning left and right:

Turn Left
Right to Go
Right to Stop

When confident with the first three, then add a few emerge left and right routines.

You will need the help of someone once you have written down three routines above, or better still if you can print them off, then they will tell you the first of these that they want you to repeat back to them, Imagine yourself driving along a road and being asked to take the next turning on the left. Once you are able to repeat the routine to turn left flawlessly, sit down on a chair, as if in the car with your hands out in front of you holding the steering wheel, close your eyes and say the routine out loud for turning left, at the same time go through all the motions of an actual left turn.

Interior
Left
Indicate
Position
Brake (Gently)
Clutch Down
2nd Gear
Clutch Up
Follow Corner Round
Gas
Check Mirror

Follow on through the gears up to 4th and when the person helping you hears 4th gear they will then ask you to carry out the next turn, maybe a right to stop, which you will repeat back to them as you do the virtual drive, followed by a right to go etc. You will run through each routine until you have done all them. After you have mastered them, then you can move on to emerge left or right, and indeed all the routines. Make sure the person asking you to turn has a copy of the routines to check how you are doing.

You can take this a step further by adding entering and leaving a roundabout, or as many manoeuvres as you like. This exercise will help develop your thought process and should assist you when it comes to doing it for real. The more you practice the more you will remember the faster you should be able to learn to drive. Give it a go it can only help and should be fun.

<u>You have now completed Exercise 13.</u>

Please be kind enough to leave me a review of my book as I rely on your comments.

Manoeuvres and their Routines

1. 3-Point Turn (Turn in the Road)

2. Parallel Parking (Reverse Parking)

3. Left Reverse Round a Corner.

4. Right Reverse Round a Corner.

5. Emergency Stop (Controlled Stop)

6. Reverse into a Parking Bay.

7. Hill Start.

Exercise 14: Three Point Turn (Turn in the Road)

The objective of this manoeuvre is to be able to turn the car round in a road and end up with the car facing the other way in the opposite lane. You would use this manoeuvre if you drove into a road that was a dead end and you had to turn round to exit, or if you found yourself heading in the wrong direction and had to turn back.

Make sure that it is carried out in a safe & convenient place to perform the manoeuvre. There is no need to indicate, as you will only proceed when there are no cars or pedestrians around. Never attempt to do a turn in the road in a main road.

(See Diagram 1)

TURN IN THE ROAD

You need to know about a couple of phrases: **'Dry Steer'** & **'Camber'**

Dry Steer: This is when you move the steering wheel when the car is stationary, this will wear down your tyre tread in one area, so wait until the car moves before steering.

Camber: Each road has camber to allow runoff of rainwater, the highest part of any road is in the middle, and if you look at the centre line in the road to the kerb you will notice there is a small incline towards the kerb. So in effect, when you start this manoeuvre, you will be going up hill and once passed the centre line you will be going down hill.

To perform this manoeuvre you need: Good clutch control, a slow car and a brisk steering with full push – pull hand movements. (No dry steer) If there are any vehicles approaching then do not go until it is clear (there is no need to indicate) if there are any people walking on the pavement opposite you wait for them to pass, this also applies for reversing.

All manoeuvres require a great deal of clutch control to move slowly and keep the car under control. I suggest before attempting this manoeuvre that you practice clutch control.

To Turn In The Road, do the following:

You need a **'Point of Stop'** for going forward and reversing; they will prevent you touching the kerb. The point of stop for going forward is when your right hand door mirror is just over the kerb. (See Picture 1)

The point of stop for reversing is when you look through your right door window, down at the bottom right corner of it (See Picture 2)

Going Forward:

POM the car, and as you move the car slowly, start turning the steering wheel to the right (brisk steering wheel, slow car) as you go halfway over the road, look to your right, for one last check for oncoming cars, then look down to your right door mirror, (See Picture 1) as the kerb begins to appear just below it, make two last turns of the wheel to the left and stop, the two turns at the end will set the cars wheels up to help when reversing. When you pass the centre white line the camber may affect your speed, put the clutch down and use the footbrake to control the car as necessary.

Picture 1. This is what you should see going forward as your point of stop.

Reversing:

After stopping, there are three things you need to do to prepare the car for reversing, foot on the brake, into reverse and up to biting point. There are now three observations that have to be made, through your right and left door windows and out the back window, looking over your left shoulder. If it's clear, then continue, otherwise, wait for it to clear, keep an eye on any vehicles that have pulled up allowing you to continue with this manoeuvre, they may decide to go, any pedestrians walking behind the car then wait till they have gone by.

As you start to go backwards, steer briskly to the left and a quick look out the back window over your left shoulder, remember to clutch up/clutch down to control the speed of the car. Remember the camber should kick after the centre line so start to clutch down and use your footbrake to slow the car. When halfway across, look to your right for your point to stop. (See Picture 2) You will see the kerb approach your point of stop, just before the kerb touches the corner of your window, turn the steering wheel twice to the right and stop, this set the cars wheels up to help when moving forward.

Picture 2. This is what you should see going reversing as your point of stop.

Note1: For the experienced driver teaching a trainee I suggest that if you find that there is a problem with the trainee hitting the kerb on reversing, you may have to establish their own point of stop. When reversing, do not stop the car but let it slowly roll back, with the clutch down and gently touch the kerb (make sure there are no trees or posts etc near the kerb that you may hit) Then select first and move forward a few feet or about ½ metre. The trainee can now look down and identify their own new point of stop, ask

them to remember this for the next time they try this.

Going Forward (Completing the manoeuvre):

Going forward there are again 3 things you need to do to prepare the car, foot on the brake, into 1st gear and up to biting point. There are now two observations that have to be made, through your right and left door windows looking forward past the experienced driver. If it's clear, then continue; otherwise, wait for it to clear, keep an eye on any vehicles that may have stopped allowing you to continue with this manoeuvre, they may decide to go just as you do. You may pull up when it's safe to do so, and repeat the process until you are satisfied that you can do it successfully.

Note2: It does not matter if instead of a 3-point turn it has to be done in a 5 turns, as this might happen due to turning in a tight road.

You have now completed a Three Point Turn.

Three Point Turn routine.

Going Forward

POM. (Prepare, Observe & Move - No indications, any people or cars then wait)
Full right lock (as you start to move) until kerb is just under the right door mirror.
Turn wheel twice left just before stopping.

3 Checks:
Into reverse.
Up to biting point.
Foot on brake.

3 Observations:
Look right.
Look left.
Look out back window.

Reversing

Full left lock (as you start to move) <u>quick</u> last look out of back window.
Kerb in bottom right of right door window.
Turn wheel twice right just before stopping.

Going Forward

3 Checks:
Into 1st.
Up to biting point.
Foot on brake.

2 Observations:

Look right then left (Round the examiner) Move off making sure that you watch any cars that have stopped for you.

Exercise 15: Reverse Parking (Parallel Park)

The objective of this manoeuvre is to be able to reverse the car safely and under full control, parking it close to the kerb. You will use this manoeuvre if you have to park in a space between two vehicles, but for your test, your examiner will only ask you to do this where there is only the one car and I suggest that you practise this way also. Dry Steer & Camber also applies here. See 'Turn In the Road'

All manoeuvres require a great deal of clutch control to move slowly and keep the car under control. I suggest before attempting this manoeuvre that you practice clutch control.

(See Diagram 1)

Diagram 1

REVERSE PARKING

The examiner will ask you to pull up behind a car that he or she will want you to perform a reverse park on. It will be about two or three cars lengths away from it, when you finish the manoeuvre you should be about 2 car lengths behind the car and close to the kerb, ideally 4 or 5 inches or 10 to 12 centimetres from the kerb.

To Parallel Park, do the following:
Position your car two or three car lengths behind the stationary vehicle that you wish to practise on. POM the car, move out and up along side the parked vehicle, about a couple of feet or ½ metre away from it. Make sure that the left indicator is on and when you stop your car, your left hand door mirror should be just past the front of the parked vehicle. (See Picture 1)

Picture 1. Stop car ½ metre away and door mirror at the end of the car.

With your foot on the brake, put your car into reverse, up to biting point. Now do your six observations again, if there are any vehicles then wait until they pass or wait behind you, allowing you to continue, but keep an eye on them, they may decide to pass you, if there are any people walking past the parked car on your left, stop and wait for them to pass.

When clcar to go, reverse slowly back, looking over your left shoulder at the back nearside (kerb-side) seatbelt until it reaches the end of the parked car. (See Picture 2)

Picture 2. Point of turn is your back seatbelt level or just past end of vehicle.

At this point turn the steering wheel one full turn to your left, look into your right hand door mirror (the car will start to swing out into the road) if you see any approaching vehicles from the front or behind then stop and let them go, after looking all round to see if it is still clear to go, continue back looking to the front and over your right shoulder, when your left hand door mirror is in line with the end of the parked vehicle start to turn the steering wheel reasonably slowly until full right lock. See Picture 3.

Picture 3. Second point of turn is when your door mirror is near the end of the vehicle.

As the car begins to get close to the kerb, look at the front of your car in relation to the parked car, and as you start to get parallel with the kerb, turn the steering wheel two turns to the left to straighten up. The car should now be parallel with the kerb. When asked to drive on, POM the car and drive on as normal.

If you found that you hit the kerb then you need to turn the steering wheel a little bit faster next time when you apply full right lock at the end of the parked car, if you were quite a distance from the kerb, then you need to turn the steering wheel more slowly full right lock, You will have to practice this manoeuvre many times until it becomes natural to you.

Note: For the experienced driver teaching a trainee I suggest that you understand this manoeuvre and perform it yourself following the above instructions before you ask the trainee to do so.

You have now completed Parallel Parking.

Routine for Parallel Park (Reverse Park)

POM. (Prepare, Observe & Move)

½ Metre from side of car, front of car will be level with your left door mirror.

Foot on brake, into reverse, left indicator on and full observations.

Reverse back until your rear seatbelt is level with end of car.

Turn wheel 1 full turn left, check right side mirror.

Left door mirror halfway down the car look over right shoulder.

When your left door mirror is level with end of car, slow full right lock.

Straighten car up when parallel with kerb, 2 turns to the left.

Exercise 16: Left Reverse Round a Corner

The objective of this manoeuvre is to be able to reverse the car safely and under full control, into an opening on the left. You will use this manoeuvre if you find yourself heading in the wrong direction and maybe in a tight road and unable to turn the car around or reversing into a driveway.

All manoeuvres require a great deal of clutch control to move slowly and keep the car under control. I suggest before attempting this manoeuvre that you practice clutch control.

(See Diagram 1)

Diagram 1

REVERSE LEFT

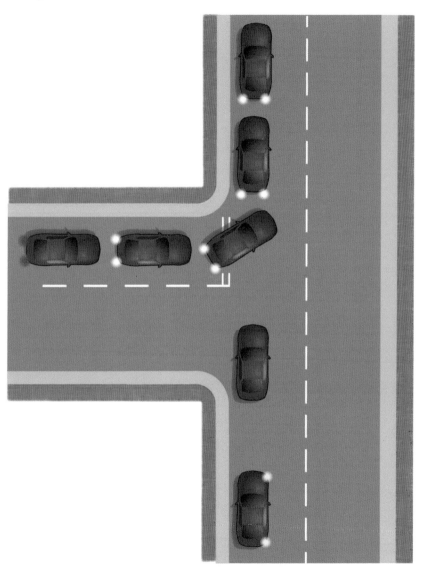

The examiner will ask you to pull up before the road that they will want you to reverse into.

To Reverse Round a Corner On The Left, do the following:

After pulling up on the left before the corner you will to reverse into, POM the car and drive slowly past the road that you will reverse into, as you go by, look into the road and look to see if there are any obstructions, how sharp the corner is, or if it is up or down hill.

Indicate left as you pass the middle white line in the road, pull up about 2 car lengths past the corner and about a drains width from the kerb, (about 12 inches or 30 centimetres) with your foot on the brake put your car into reverse and up to biting point. Now do six observations again, if there are any vehicles approaching in either direction then stop until they pass, if there are any people walking close to the road you intend to reverse into, stop and wait for them to clear.

When clear to go, reverse slowly (making sure that the steering wheel is straight) looking out for any vehicles that may be approaching, if you see one then stop the car when it gets near you until it is clear to continue. (If you do stop make sure you do all your observations again) Reverse back until your 'Point of Turn' is where the kerb in the road you wish to reverse into, is in line with the bottom corner of your rear kerbside window. (See Picture 1)

Picture 1. Point of turn is where you see the kerb in left back side window.

Then slow full left lock as you continue to move the car round the corner. (You will have to turn the steering wheel relative to the sharpness of the corner if it is a sweeping corner) The front of your car is now beginning to swing out into the road so continue to look for oncoming vehicles and stop if necessary.

When you are nearly round and it is clear to continue, look over your left shoulder through the back window for the kerb appearing in the new road, (See Picture 2)

As soon as you see it, keep the steering wheel full left lock, look into your left hand door mirror, you will see the kerb and car getting closer in that mirror, just before you get to the desired distance, turn your steering wheel two turns to your right, this will straighten up the wheel and you should be going straight back. If when you are nearly round you think that you will hit the kerb, then stop and move the car forward a little, then continue to reverse again.

Picture 2. Point of turn is where you see the kerb in left back side window.

If you are too close or too far away from the kerb as you go back then you might need slight adjustments as you go, if you are too far away from the kerb then turn the steering wheel to your left, if you are quite close to the kerb then turn to your right. You can stop at any time for all manoeuvres to carry out observations. Continue backwards making full observations as you go, do not stare into your left hand door mirror but glance at it every now and again to make any corrections.

Stop when you are about 2 to 3 cars lengths back and secure the car. When asked to drive on, POM the car and drive on. If a vehicle was to drive up behind you as you are reversing into the new road, then tell the examiner that you are going to abandon this manoeuvre, drive forward and start it again.

Note1: Never reverse a vehicle into a main road.

You have now completed Left Reverse Round A Corner.

Routine for Left reverse round a corner

POM. (Prepare, Observe & Move)

Drive past the road and indicate as you pass the white line.

Stop a drain's distance from the kerb, 2 to 3 car lengths from corner.

Foot on brake, into reverse, kill the indicator and full observations.

Reverse back to point of turn, any cars or pedestrians, stop.

Slow full left turn with observations, any cars or pedestrians, stop.

¾ way round look thru back window, see kerb, look into left door mirror.

Gap slowly reduces; No Steering until just before the desired width.

Turn wheel twice to straighten up, adjust wheel if necessary.

Full observations on the way back.

Exercise 17: Right Reverse Round a Corner

The objective of this manoeuvre is to be able to reverse the car safely and under full control, into an opening on the right. Your examiner may ask you to perform a right reverse round a corner, but normally they ask you to perform a left turn, so you will have to practice doing this.

The examiner will ask you to pull up on the left side of the road, just before the road on the right that they will want you to reverse into.

To Reverse Round a Corner To The Right, do the following:

POM the car and as you drive past the road you wish to reverse in to, indicate right, after the middle white line of that road. As you go by, look into the road and look to see if there are any obstructions, how sharp the corner is, or if it is up or down hill.

Pull up on the right when safe to do so about 2 car lengths past the corner and about a drain's width from the kerb, (about 12 inches or 30 centimetres) apply the footbrake and put your car into reverse, and up to biting point. Now do six observations again, if there are any vehicles approaching in either direction then stop until they pass, if there are any people walking close to the road you intend to reverse into, stop and wait for them to clear.

When clear to go, reverse slowly (making sure that the steering wheel is straight) looking for any vehicles that are approaching, if you see one then stop the car until it is clear to continue. Reverse back until your 'Point of Turn' which in this case is where the kerb in the road you wish to reverse into is in line with the bottom corner of your rear nearside window (similar to left reverse round a corner) then slowly turn the steering wheel in relation to the sharpness of the corner, use your right door mirror to follow the corner round, but remember full observations as you go.

The front of your car is now beginning to swing out into the road so continue to look for oncoming vehicles and stop if necessary.

If you are too close or too far away from the kerb as you go back then you might need slight adjustments as you go, if you are too far away from the kerb then turn the steering wheel to your right, if you are quite close to the kerb then turn to your left. Continue backwards making full observations as you go, do not stare into your right hand door mirror but glance at it every now and again to make any corrections. Stop when you are about 5 cars lengths back (or five white lines in that road) and secure the car.

The reason you go back so far, is if a vehicle turns into the road you are reversing down, your car will be back far enough back for them to avoid you. When asked to drive on, POM the car and drive on, moving over to the left hand lane.

<u>You have now completed Right Reverse Round A Corner.</u>

Routine for Right reverse round a corner

POM. (Prepare, Observe & Move)

Drive past the road and indicate as you pass the white line.

Stop a drain's distance from the kerb, 2 to 3 car lengths from corner.

Foot on brake, into reverse, kill the indicator and full observations.

Reverse back to point of turn, any cars or pedestrians, stop.

Slow full right turn with observations, any cars or pedestrians, stop.

Gap slowly reduces; No Steering until just before the desired width.

Turn wheel twice to straighten up, adjust wheel if necessary.

Full observations on the way back.

Stop after the five white lines.

Exercise 18: Emergency Stop (Controlled Stop)

The objective of this manoeuvre is to perform an emergency stop, promptly and under full control.

To Perform an Emergency Stop, do the following:

1. Do not check any mirrors.
2. Keep both hands firmly on the wheel.
3. Have a quick reaction.
4. Brake progressively and firmly.
5. Put the clutch down before stopping.
6. Secure the car and drive on when told to.

This is an explanation of the 6 points above:

1. You will not have time to check any mirrors in an emergency.

2. Keep both hands firmly on the wheel at all times, this may prevent you from skidding as holding the wheel with one hand could force you in to a skid, as you brake hard.

3. A quick reaction has to do with being fit to drive, if you are tired or even taking sleeping aids then you should not be driving, as your responses will be slower.

4. Do not brake too hard so that the car screeches to a halt. If you skid, ease off the brakes and apply more gently.

5. If you put the clutch down at the same time as you brake then the car will be moving faster, this is because there is no engine braking taking place. (See Exercise 3 Coasting & Engine Braking) With some cars you can do both at the same time, you should refer to your car manual to check this.

6. Handbrake on, 1st gear, biting point, cover the clutch, 6 observations, and move on when told do so, <u>do not forget that last quick look right as you start to move.</u>

Now try running through the process by the side of the road a few times so that you can get used to the routine, and when you are ready to try it when driving, find a quite straight road, and clear all objects from the back seat that could be propelled through to the front of the car. The experienced driver must check in their rear mirror (if they have one) and a quick look out of the back window, that it's clear to perform the controlled stop. Try doing for the first time in first gear to see how it feels, then move on to third gear and eventually forth.

After you have completed the controlled stop, the examiner (or the experienced driver) will say 'Drive on when you are ready'. If you are happy or have teaching this exercise, say 'Thank you, I will not be asking you to do that again'. We have to let the trainee know that we have finished with that exercise, and if you happen to mention STOP in further conversations then hopefully they will not perform a controlled stop out of the blue.

ABS:

Most new cars come fitted with ABS braking, this stands for 'Anti-Locking Braking System' The ABS system detects when a car wheel starts to lock-up (which can cause the car to skid) and momentarily releases it and re-engages it many time a second. This will allow a car to steer round an object as it braked hard towards it.

If you do not have ABS and find yourself in a skid, then if the back of your car starts to swing round, either to the left or right, then counteract this by steering in the opposite direction of the swing.

You have now completed an Emergency Stop.

Routine for Emergency Stop (Controlled Stop)

When asked to perform a emergency stop:

Brake (Progressively & Firmly)

Put clutch down before stopping.

Handbrake on.

In to 1st gear, (left hand back on handbrake)

Up to biting point.

Cover gas.

Full observations and last check to your right as you move off.

Exercise 19: Bay Reverse Parking into a Bay

The objective of this manoeuvre is to be able to reverse the car safely and under full control into a parking bay. You will use this manoeuvre if you have to park in a car park.

All manoeuvres require a great deal of clutch control to move slowly and keep the car under control. I suggest before attempting this manoeuvre that you practice clutch control.

To reverse into a Parking Bay (To The Right) do the following:

Pick a place where there are no parked cars near where you intend to practise this exercise. Move up along side the bay that you wish to reverse into and go past it, about 2 bay lengths. Apply the footbrake, put your car into reverse and up to biting point. Now do your six observations again, if there are any people walking past you, then wait for them to pass, keep alert at all times while reversing.

Your point of turn is your car door opener, (See Picture 1)

Picture 1.Point of turn is where you see the white line level with door opener.

Set the car up so that the door opener is in line
with any white bay line on your right, or as you
can see the white line is just under the door
mirror, as you go back, when you see the next
white bay line become level with your door
opener, as in the illustration, start to turn the
steering wheel briskly to you right, make full
observations as you go back, when ¾ of the way
round, check your left hand door mirror, you
should see the white bay line of the bay you wish
to reverse into appear in it, at this point, turn the
steering wheel twice to your left, to straighten up.
(See Picture 2)

Picture 2. White bay line in left door mirror slowly start to straighten up car.

You should now be going straight back into the bay, keep observing as you go back. Your point to stop would be when the line across the front of the bay is just under your door mirror, or when you get close to a vehicle that may be parked in bay behind you. The front of the vehicle behind you may be just inside your bay, so check your interior mirror. (See Picture 3)

Picture 3. Your point to stop would be when the line across the front of the bay is just under your door mirror, or maybe the vehicle behind you.

For bay parking on the left, follow the routine above with the opposite reference points. Try this manoeuvre on a quite day, when the car park is less full of cars.

Note: For the experienced driver teaching a trainee I suggest that you understand this manoeuvre and perform it yourself before you ask the trainee to do so.

You have now completed bay reverse parking.

Routine to Reverse into a Parking Bay

POM. (Prepare the car in reverse, Observe & Move)

White bay line level with door handle.

Full right lock of steering wheel, at point of turn.

Full observations on way back.

¾ way round, check left door mirror.

When left bay white line appears in the mirror, turn wheel twice.

If you have a problem move forward and then reverse in to bay.

Reverse with observations till bay line is just under door mirror.

Be aware the point of stop may be the car parked behind,
check interior mirror.

Exercise 20: Hill Start

The objective of this manoeuvre is to move off uphill and downhill.

To Perform a Hill Start, do the following:

Uphill

When asked to pull over when driving up a hill, remember that the car will slow down a lot faster than if you were pulling up on level ground. If you slow down and stop short of being close to the kerb, then you may need to select first gear and pull the car in closer to the kerb.

When you have pulled up, make sure you secure the handbrake firmly. You will then be asked to move off when you are ready, POM the car as normal and when you bring the clutch up to biting point (make sure you can feel biting point) apply a little bit more gas than normal, release the handbrake, and move off in the normal manner. Again make sure you are at biting point before you release the handbrake and with the gas bring up the clutch slowly as the car starts to move up hill. Gear changing going up hill will be slightly longer, as the car can struggle to get moving, so don't change gear too soon.

Downhill

When asked to pull over when driving down a hill, the car will be braking under the gravity of the hill, so you might have to start slowing down earlier than if you were pulling up on level ground.

When you have pulled up, make sure you secure the handbrake <u>firmly</u>. You will then be asked to move off when you are ready, POM the car as normal, but this time when preparing the car, after selecting first gear, **<u>do not</u>** bring the clutch up to biting point (as gravity will make the car move of) release the handbrake, and move off with your clutch fully down until the car starts to move, then slowly bring up the clutch. For really steep hills, select second gear instead of first and do the above.

<u>**You have now completed Hill Start and the last of your manoeuvres.**</u>

Please be kind enough to leave me a review of my book as I rely on your comments.

Exercise 21: Show Me Tell Me

At the start of your practical test and after the examiner has checked your documents and your eyesight, the examiner will ask you two basic maintenance questions, they may ask you to open the bonnet of the car and ask one or two questions regarding to what's under the bonnet, or indeed both questions could be to do with operational instruments within the car. They will consist of a 'Show me' question and/or a 'Tell me' question. If you fail to answer one or both of these questions correctly then you will receive one minor fault.

The questions that you could be asked are as follows:

Show Me:

Q.   Show me how you would check power steering is working properly before moving off.
A.   With your left hand, apply some pressure on the steering wheel, then start the car, you should then feel and see the power steering kick in.

Q.   Show me how you would check the cars horn is working properly.
A.   Point at the horn and explain, do not press it unless asked to do so.

Q.   Show me how you would check the parking brake (Hand Brake) for excessive wear.
A.   Put your foot on the foot brake to secure the car, release the handbrake & reapply, it should feel tight and if it comes up to far then there's a problem with it.

Q.   Show me how you would check the indicators are working properly.
A.   Turn on the hazard warning lights and walk round the car, checking all indicators, including the side indicators. (Do not walk in the road)

Q.   Show me how you would check the cars headlights and taillights are working properly.
A.   Turn on the car lights and walk round the car, checking all lights. (Do not walk in the road)

Tell Me:

Q.   Tell me how you would check that the cars brake lights are working properly.
A.   Put your foot on the footbrake then ask someone to check them or use reflections on garage door or windows.

Q.   Tell me how you would check the car brakes are working.

A.   They should not feel spongy or slack, you should test them just as you start to move off and they shouldn't pull to one side.

Q.   Tell me how you would check the cars tyres, for tread depth and general condition.
A.   There should be no cuts or bulges with a minimum of 1.6mm of tread across the central width of the tyre and all the way round. (Use tyre gauge to check)

Q.   Tell me where you would find the information for the recommended tyre pressure for your car.
A.   You would check in the car manufactures book that came with the car.

You will have to open the car bonnet for the next set of questions.

Q.   How would you check the brake fluid bottle so that it has a safe level of brake fluid in it?
A.   Point to the brake fluid bottle and show the min/max marks, this is where the level should be between.

Q.   How would you check the car's engine oil level?
A.   When the engine is cold, take out the dipstick, clean it, put it back in for a few seconds,

pull it out again, and there should be oil between the min/max levels. If there were no oil between the min/max levels then I would add some oil a bit at a time, and repeat the process.

Q.   How would you check the engine coolant level and if it was at the correct level?
A.   Point to the engine coolant bottle and show the min/max marks; this is where the level should be between. If you have to fill it up with water then wait for the engine to be cool down.

Q.   Where is the windscreen water bottle?
A.   Point to the windscreen water bottle and mention that you would check it weekly and if it's nearly empty you would refill it.

You must remember all these questions/answers, open up the bonnet of the car every now and again and make sure that you know each answer.

You have now completed Exercise 21.

Please be kind enough to leave me a review of my book as I rely on your comments.

Exercise 22: Taking the Theory Test

If you have not passed your theory test, or at least started on it, then I suggest that you do so as soon as possible as this will help you before driving out in the open road.

The things that I suggest you buy would be:

The Highway Code.
A Book of Road Signs.
The Official Driving Test.
Hazard Perception CD-ROM. (HPT)

Watch the DSA video on YouTube: http: //youtu.be/z_zi6j24F6s

The Highway Code has everything to do with the road and other users.
A book of road signs will show you all signs that you may encounter.
The official driving test is everything you need to know about the practical test.
The HPT will have sample video clips the theory test questions.

The Theory test consists of two parts, multiple-choice questions and answers, and HPT (Hazard perception Test) where you are shown video clips. You must pass both the multiple choice and the hazard perception tests in order to pass your theory.

When you arrive for your theory test, get there early so you won't feel rushed and that you can relax before it. You will need to take your provisional licence, counterpart driving licence (the green piece of paper that came with your photo licence) and your test appointment letter. Remember to take both parts of your provisional licence or you will not be able to take the test. If you have booked at short notice then you should give your booking number. If you have an older type licence you will have to bring a valid passport.

You will be asked to turn off your mobile phone if you have one, You will not be allowed to take anything in to the test with you, so you will be asked to place all your personal belongings in to a locker, take a key, and then take a seat and wait to be called.

When you are called, your details will be checked again to ensure that you are taking the correct test. You will then be told to go to a workstation where there will be a PC, you will be asked to confirm that it is your name that is on the screen, do so if it is correct, then press start, you will then see an introduction screen that tells you how the test works.

Multiple-choice:

For the multiple-choice section you have the option of a practise session, so take full advantage of this and do it. It will last for 15 minutes and does not count towards your actual test. There is a clock at the top of the screen that will tell how much time is left.

Some questions have more than one answer, if you do not choose enough answers a message will flash to inform you to select more, the time allowed for the multiple-choice part is 57 minutes, so relax and take your time. In order to pass this part of the test you must answer a 43 out of the 50 questions correctly.

After completing the multiple choice test you will have up to three minutes until you start the hazard perception test, you can wait and have a rest in that time or you can start it straight away.

Hazard Perception:

There are 14 hazard perception video clips each lasting around 1 minute, with 15 developing hazards so there is one hazard in each clip, one of the clips will have 2 hazards, so watch each one carefully. The test should last around 20 minutes. You will be asked to put the headphones on so that you can listen while you watch an explanation of this part of the test.

This section deals with you being able to scan the road ahead for possible hazards and how you react to each of them as and when they develop. In each clip there are hazards just like those you will see in the road, some will start to develop and these are the ones that might cause a driver to slow down or change direction.

It could be a cyclist, a pedestrian walking into the road, an emerging car (from either your left or right) someone approaching a pedestrian crossing etc. <u>Keep alert</u>.

You will be tested on how you respond to the developing hazards and given points for how soon you spotted them. 5 points will be given for spotting them on time, down through to 0 for those that are spotted too late or missed altogether. Each time you click a red flag appears at the bottom of the screen to show you that your click has been registered. If you click too much you not score anything for that clip, so think before you click.

In order to pass this part of the test you will have to score a minimum of 44 points out of 75 to pass it.

On completed of the test, go to the reception, take your personal belongings out of the locker and wait for your results, this should take a few minutes. After you have successfully passed your Theory test, you will have two years in which to pass your Practical test.

When you are ready to take your theory test call the DSA and they will give the next available date, time and location suitable to where you live that suits you.

Exercise 23: Taking the Practical Test

For the test you will be required to bring the necessary documents with you:

Provisional Driving Licence (Photo Id)
Provisional Driving Licence Your Theory test pass certificate.
The letter the DSA sent you confirming your test date.

If you have an older type licence you will have to bring a valid passport.

When you have booked a date for your practical test, the DSA (Driving Standards Agency) will send you confirmation of the date, location of the test centre and at what time the test will take place.

If after booking your test, feel unready for that particular test date, then you can call the DSA and ask them for the next available date. This must be done 3 working days prior to your actual test date; this date is also on the confirmation form. You will lose your money if you cancel or try to postpone after this date. On doing this, the DSA will send you confirmation of your new test date; you must keep this document, as you will need it for your test.

If you are not taking your test with an ADI and, then the car that you are using must be insured for the test, have a small mirror for the examiner to see behind him and L-Plates displayed on the front and back of it.

The test will last for roughly 35-40 minutes and in that time they will first check all four documents (see above) confirm that you live at the same address that is on your provisional licence and ask you to sign, saying that the car is insured for the test itself. If you wish for your instructor to accompany you on test, which you are entitled to do so, then this is the time to ask. They examiner will then check your eyesight (see Exercise 1: cockpit drill & controls) and then ask you to walk to your car and may ask you to open up the bonnet and you will be asked two 'Show me Tell me' questions, either to do with under the bonnet or functionality within the car. (See Exercise 14)

When you have started to drive, the examiner will inform you in good time as to where to go and what they require you to do, so just follow the road ahead until asked to change direction or pull up. You will be asked to perform one of the manoeuvres that you have learned in this course, and you may also be asked to 'pull up and then move off' again a number of times; the examiner will be watching where you pull up to see if you pull up on a bend, or maybe opposite a junction, so think before you do pull up, there is no rush to do so just because they have asked you, find some where safe.

They will be assessing you overall driving skills, your ability to carry out manoeuvres safely and how safe a driver you are. The examiner will also ask you to follow a predetermined route that will allow them to access your independent driving skills, this is usually a diagram that they show you or ask you to follow that particular route using traffic signs, this part of the test should last around 10 minutes. If you feel that you have made a mistake during your test, do not panic, keep calm and get on with the rest of the test, you might find that it wasn't as bad as you thought.

In order to pass your test you have to score up to 15 or less minor faults (but no serious or dangerous faults) more than this and you will fail, regardless of how you performed your manoeuvres. Overall the examiner will be looking to see if you are a safe, confident and courteous driver. At the end of the test the will add up all the minor faults that occurred during your test and inform you if you have passed or failed.

If you pass or fail your test, it is advisable for you not to drive home because you will be either very happy or sad, either way you will not be able to concentrate on driving and this could be very dangerous for yourself and other road users.

When you go for your practical test, get there about 10 minutes beforehand so you won't feel rushed and you can relax before it, if you arrive too early it may interfere with those tests that started before yours. **Please remember to <u>turn off</u> your mobile phone before the test.**

I can only remind you again that when you start your test that you recall all your routines that you have learnt for each particular part of the driving, apply them fully and they will see you through your test successfully. **Good luck on the Day.**

Note: When you have passed your test you will be on probation period for two years, if you get 6 penalty points within that time then you will have to retake your theory and practical test again.

<u>STAY ALERT & SAFE DRIVING FOR LIFE</u>

Please be kind enough to leave me a review of my book as I rely on your comments.

Other books you might like to buy:

Learn To Drive (General Driving)
http://www.amazon.co.uk/dp/B0074B6NOK#_

Or if you would like to get all the Manoeuvres, General Driving & so much more on learning to drive in one complete book then purchase:

Learn To Drive (All the Manoeuvres)
http://www.amazon.co.uk/dp/B0074B3AVY#_